©2024 Kimberly L. Suber and Kai A. Suber
All rights reserved.
Book Cover and Illustration by: Kreative Artz
Published by: Kai and Mimi's Adventures
info@kaiandmimi.org
Kai's Brainventure with Mimi
ISBN: 979-8-9903372-0-6
Ebook ISBN: 979-8-9903372-1-3

Hey there, I'm Kai, and brace yourselves for an exciting adventure with my MiMi! She says we're on a mission to flex my brain muscles and turning me into a little genius!

Let's rewind to the time when I was just a tiny baby, Mimi shared sweet secrets with me, whispering, "We're nurturing your Amazing Brain." Although I could barely see her, her voice sounded magical, almost like she had a direct connection to my little brain.

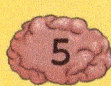

Mimi has this interesting concept that the brain acts as a "social organ." Her goal is to ensure my sense of security, and the key to this approach is forming connections.

It's heartwarming when we snuggle, and she draws near, revealing her twinkling eyes. Mimi mentions it's about "programming my brain with love and safety" through a superhero ability known as neuroplasticity. Indeed, superheroes have the ability to influence and sculpt your brain!

I believe Mimi is my superhero because she engages in conversations and laughter with me. While I attempt to communicate, all I can do is blow bubbles. Mimi refers to this as building "emotional glue," envisioning it as a unique invisible bond that binds us together. One thing is certain: I enjoy spending time with Mimi and sharing my brightest smiles with everyone around us.

Stepping into Mimi's cozy world feels like entering the safest place ever. She lays out soft blankets and toys, and I showcase my magical leg maneuvers known as "scooting" and "crawling." It's similiar to exploring a magical world! Every tiny scoot and crawl shows a sense of security within Mimi's nurturing environment.

But if I take a tumble, my tiny brain freaks out. Mimi says it goes downstairs into a fight, flight, freeze, or fawn stage. I'm just a baby, okay? But Mimi talks to me, and suddenly, it's all cool. We even practice breathing, but I always end up giggling. Mimi says my brain is back upstairs, and I'm ready to explore again.

Mimi introduce a mysterious world of giant numbers and letter puzzles, making it feel like a top-secret language lesson. It's like she's throwing a party for my logical left brain! Using the right side of my brain, helps me express emotions, play, enjoy Mimi's songs, and let my imagination run wild with blocks. I can easily identify Mimi in any room. Seeing her face activates my right brain and provides me with a strong sense of security.

Mimi reveals an intersting box filled with vibrant colors and shapes, named "peek-a-boo box," that excites me as it opens and closes. It's as if a party for my brain is hidden inside a box. Mimi says it's not just any box; it's a magical journey for my mind, keeping me happy and entertained!

At times, I sprinkle some wisdom during chats, and Mimi totally vibes with the baby talk. She's all in for boosting my brainpower, hinting that hey, mayb one day I'll be the President of the United States.

Mimi's all about creating awesome memories with me. With my brain sizzling with "implicit memories," I'm on the fast lane to becoming a brainiac with a squad of pals, all thanks to Mimi.

READY TO LEARN

EXCITED

She mentioned she would ensure I'am "regulated." Big word alert! However, I understand she is being a superhero by ensuring I feel secure even in her absence. This helps me stay calm and have the most fantastic days!

Glossary of Terminology for Parents

- **Downstairs Brain:** The foundational part of the brain responsible for managing emotions and vital functions such as breathing. It triggers responses like fight, flight, freeze, or fold.

- **Explicit Memory:** The ability to recall facts and skills, such as remembering a phone number or mathematical procedures.

- **Implicit Memory:** Memories derived from experiences that influence or shape our emotional responses.

- **Left Brain:** The analytical hemisphere of the brain involved in language development, reasoning, and the retention of factual information.

- **Neuroplasticity:** The brain's remarkable capacity to adapt, change, and form new neural connections.

- **Regulated:** The process of managing and responding to emotions effectively.

- **Right Brain:** The creative and intuitive hemisphere of the brain that fosters social interaction, imagination, motor skills, and exploration.

- **Social Organ:** The brain's need for social interactions, such as smiles and hugs, as it is inherently wired for social engagement.

- **Stimulating Activity:** Engaging and interactive experiences that aim to captivate and stimulate a child's senses, curiosity, and cognitive abilities.

- **Upstairs Brain:** The prefrontal cortex responsible for executive functions, preparing the brain for learning and higher-order thinking.

That's just the beginning of my Amazing Brainventure! The excitement doesn't end here. Mimi and I have a multitude of thrilling adventures waiting to unfold.

Look out for upcoming books on
Kai's Adventures to Understanding:

- Understanding No
- Emotions
- Self-Awareness
- Self-Management
- Social Awareness
- Responsible Decision Making
- Relationship Skills

About the Authors

Kai Ashton Suber, widely recognized as Boss Baby, derives great joy from acquiring cognitive strategies under the guidance of his exceptional Mimi. Known for his infectious smile and exuberant expressions of delight upon each new discovery, Kai's enthusiasm resonates across the cosmos.

With an extensive background spanning over two decades in the field of education, Ms. Kimberly L. Suber has seamlessly transitioned through various roles, from teacher, to assistant principal, district administrator, and consultant. Ms. Suber stands as the visionary behind frameworks and methodologies dedicated to fostering academic motivation in children while addressing their Social and Emotional Learning requirements.

An ardent advocate of employing a positive behavior model supported by clear and consistent expectations to cultivate a secure educational environment, Ms. Suber envisions a setting where every child progresses towards their social and academic objectives. She ardently contributes to initiatives aimed at instigating positive transformations within educational institutions, benefiting all stakeholders involved.

Beyond her educational endeavors, Ms. Suber's influence extends to national and local conferences, notable publications, and interviews conducted by renowned authors seeking insights into her pedagogical practices.

www.ingramcontent.com/pod-product-compliance
Lightning Source LLC
LaVergne TN
LVHW070838080426
835510LV00030B/3447